Highlights

ALL ABOUT THE PLANET

Kid Tested by
Owen McAfee
Age 5

HIGHLIGHTS PRESS
Honesdale, Pennsylvania

Welcome to THE OCEAN

Splish-splash! Ocean water covers most of our planet. An ocean is a big, deep body of salt water. Winds help create waves on its surface. And animals such as sharks, whales, and sea turtles glide under the water. **Ready for some ocean fun? Let's dive in!**

Ocean Names
The ocean is divided into five areas:
- The Atlantic Ocean
- The Pacific Ocean
- The Arctic Ocean
- The Indian Ocean
- The Southern Ocean

Ollie's Ocean Garden

Oscar is meeting his friend Ollie. Can you help him find a path to Ollie's ocean garden?

Octopuses have three hearts.

Finish

Start

Octopuses can change color.

Sailing Sights

Bryce, Brianna, and Bettina are sailing the seas.
Find the eight hidden objects in this scene.

Jellyfish don't have brains!

A group of jellyfish is called a smack.

Art by Laura Watson

closed umbrella

ruler

piece of popcorn

cookie

button

baseball

hot dog

banana

Ocean Words

Trace the letters to write the names of five things you might find in the ocean.

Wave

Sand

Fish

Whale

Coral

Under the Sea

What silly things do you see in this watery scene?

Why Is the Sea Salty?

The ocean is very salty. Much of this salt comes from land. When rain falls, it washes salt from the land into rivers and streams. The rivers and streams carry the salt to the ocean.

Art by Gareth Lucas

Similar Seahorses

Can you find a match for each seahorse?

To keep from drifting off, seahorses may use their tails to grip seaweed.

Art by Gareth Lucas

Shark Puppet

Sharks are a type of fish. Many kinds of sharks glide through the ocean. Build your own shark puppet!

You Need
- Scissors
- Short cardboard tube
- 2-foot-long piece of yarn
- Craft stick
- Markers
- Cardstock
- Tape

Cut a notch in the top and bottom of both sides of the tube.

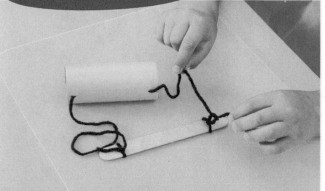

Pull the yarn halfway through the tube. Tie each end to a craft stick.

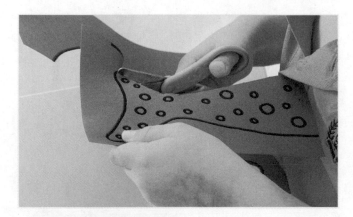

Draw a shark head, tail, and three fins on cardstock. Cut them out.

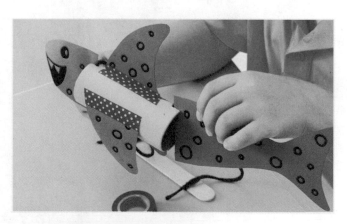

Tape on the fins. Slide the head and tail into the notches.

Deep Dive

Who will make it to the ocean floor first?
Follow each path to see which place each diver comes in.

The Mariana Trench in the Pacific Ocean is the deepest spot on Earth.

Art by Tim Budgen

Draw a Fish

Follow the steps to learn how to sketch a fish.

More Ocean Fun!

 USE YOUR STICKERS for this activity.

Anglerfish

Starfish

Whale

Dolphin

Crab

Octopus

Shark

Meet some animals you might see in the ocean. Match your stickers in the back of the book to the correct pictures here.

Lobster

Sea Turtle

Sea Otter

Manatee

Seahorse

Jellyfish

Coral

Stingray

Pufferfish

When threatened, pufferfish swell to look bigger.

Welcome to THE FOREST

Forests are filled with trees. Different kinds of forests grow across the planet. Some go through all four seasons—winter, spring, summer, and fall. Others are mostly cold and have trees with needle-shaped leaves. And still others are hot and damp. **Let's visit some forests!**

Forests cover about one-third of Earth's land surface.

Some forests have trees that grow to be the size of skyscrapers!

Art by Tim Beaumont

Fox Frenzy

These foxes are playing hide-and-seek in the forest!
Find the eight hidden objects in this scene.

Art by Laura Zarrin

recorder

flashlight

fishhook

duster

fork

fried egg

fan

fish

Red foxes can curl up and place their bushy tails over their bodies to keep warm.

Forest Critter Patterns

Find and circle each pattern below in the grid.

1.

2.

3.

Art by Rob McClurkan

Leaf Animals

Use your imagination to make forest animals from leaves!

You Need
- Leaves
- White paint
- Black paint
- Paintbrush
- Construction paper
- Glue

1 Collect.

Collect and press leaves with different shapes and colors.

2 Paint.

Paint parts of the leaf white. Let dry. Use black paint to add details.

3 Fold.

Fold construction paper into a card.

4 Glue.

Glue your leaf animal onto the card.

Forest Boogie

Some mushrooms glow in the dark.

Raccoons are mostly active at night.

It's a forest dance party! Can you find at least 11 differences between these two pictures?

Art by Andi Butler

Some groups of fireflies flash light in unison—that means together, at the exact same time.

Owls can turn their heads almost all the way around.

More Forest Fun!

USE YOUR STICKERS for this activity.

Red Fox

Bee

Squirrel

Bat

Hedgehog

Hedgehogs can have more than 5,000 spines.

Owl

Meet some animals you might see in the forest. Match your stickers in the back of the book to the correct pictures here.

Blue Jay

Skunk

Some types of skunks do handstands before spraying.

Rabbit

Turkey

Snail

Chipmunk

Beaver

Raccoon

Welcome to THE RAINFOREST

A jaguar pads along a forest floor. High above, monkeys swing from trees, and parrots call into the warm air. This is a rainforest. It's a type of forest that gets lots of . . . well . . . rain! Some rainforests grow in cooler areas. But most grow in spots that are hot and steamy. **Let's tour the rainforest!**

The largest rainforest in the world is the Amazon rainforest in South America.

Scientists think some 2.5 million species of insects live in the Amazon rainforest.

Sloth Swing

Milo the monkey found the perfect place to sit—on top of Sammy the sloth! Find the eight hidden objects in this rainforest scene.

Sloths can fall asleep hanging from a tree branch.

Anteaters slurp up ants with their sticky tongues.

sailboat

ice-cream cone

stocking

party hat

heart

star

pitcher

table-tennis paddle

Art by Nuno Alexandre Vieira

Parrot Party

Each parrot here shares a similar pattern with another parrot in the scene. Find as many matching patterns as you can.

Some parrots' beaks are strong enough to crush the world's toughest nuts.

Art by Maarten Lenoir

Draw a Monkey

Follow the steps to learn how to sketch a monkey.

Iguana Ice Cream

Isabelle is ready for a snack after a long day of traveling. Can you help her find a path through the rainforest to the ice-cream stand?

Start

Finish

Green iguanas are good swimmers.

Rainforest Words

Trace the letters to write the names of
five things you might find in the rainforest.

Tree

Flower

Rain

Bird

Insect

Butterfly Besties

Dragonflies can fly forward, backward, and upside down!

The jaguar has the strongest bite of any big cat.

This blue morpho butterfly is visiting with her rainforest friends. Can you find at least 10 differences between these two pictures?

Art by John Netz

An adult blue morpho's wingspan can be about the length of a number 2 pencil.

Flower Power

All kinds of flowers grow in the rainforest.
Can you find the two flowers below that are exactly the same?

A rainforest plant known as the "monster flower" gives off a stinky scent to attract insects.

Rainforests are home to more than half the world's plant species.

Art by Clay Cantrell

Make Your Own Flowers

Create beautiful blooms out of materials around your home!

You Need
- Cupcake liners
- Glue
- Mini baking liners
- Pompoms
- Paper straws

1 Glue.

Dab glue onto the center of the cupcake liner.

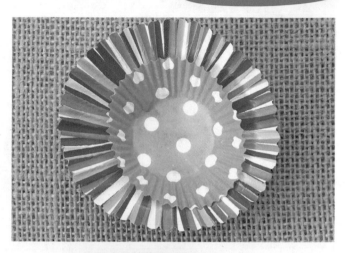

2 Layer.

Layer the mini liner onto the cupcake liner.

3 Glue.

Glue a pompom in the center of the liners.

4 Flatten.

Flatten the top of the straw. Add glue. Put the flower on top.

More Rainforest Fun!

USE YOUR STICKERS for this activity.

Frog

Monkey

Blue Morpho Butterfly

Parrot

Tiger

Jaguar

No two tigers have the same pattern of stripes.

Meet some animals you might see in the rainforest. Match your stickers in the back of the book to the correct pictures here.

Green Iguana

Chameleon

King cobras are the only snakes that build nests for their eggs.

King Cobra

Toucan

Sloth

Gorilla

Welcome to THE DESERT

A desert is an area that gets very little rain. Some deserts are hot. Others are cold. Some have mountains or sand dunes. Others are mostly flat. Deserts can be harsh places to live. Even so, lots of plants and animals thrive in these spots. **Let's head to the desert!**

Famous Deserts
- The Sahara in Africa
- The Gobi in Asia
- The Atacama in South America
- The Mojave in North America
- The Arabian in the Middle East

Art by Mike Moran

Sand and Sun

A jackrabbit is causing a ruckus at this desert campsite! Find the eight hidden objects in this scene.

A jackrabbit is a hare. Hares are related to rabbits, but are larger and have longer ears.

yo-yo

ice-cream cone

doughnut

light bulb

hammer

fish

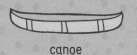

hot dog

canoe

Art by Kelly Kennedy

Desert Delights

Death Valley in California is one of the hottest deserts on Earth.

When threatened, three-banded armadillos can curl into a tight ball to stay safe.

Art by Katie McDee

Lizards, Lizards, Lizards

This desert is crawling with lizards. How many *L*'s can you find?
How many lizards do you see?

Some species, or types, of lizards do push-ups to get the attention of other lizards!

Art by Richard Johnson

Reptile Route

Help this lizard find the right path to its friends. Then color in the picture.

Start

There are thousands of species, or types, of lizards.

Finish

Art by Linda Davick

Desert Games

Why Are Cactuses Spiky?

Some types of cactuses have prickly needles. They keep hungry animals from munching on the plants. They also help shade cactuses from the sun.

These desert animals are competing to win the cactus ring toss!
Can you find at least 11 differences between these two pictures?

Art by Joey Ellis

Desert tortoises spend most of their time in underground burrows.

Some birds dig holes into cactuses to make nests.

More Desert Fun!

USE YOUR STICKERS for this activity.

Camel

Camels have superlong eyelashes to keep sand out of their eyes.

Scorpion

Snake

Meerkat

Coyote

Jackrabbit

Meet some animals you might see in the desert. Match your stickers in the back of the book to the correct pictures here.

Armadillo

Roadrunner

Turkey Vulture

Fennec Fox

Turkey vultures can smell a meal from over a mile away.

Desert Tortoise

Bobcat

Welcome to
≡ THE POLAR REGIONS ≡

The polar regions are on the very top and bottom of Earth. The top area is called the Arctic. Much of it is covered by the Arctic Ocean. The bottom area is called Antarctica. It's a huge mass of land. These spots are cold and icy. **Let's explore the polar regions!**

Antarctica may be cold and icy, but it rarely gets rain or snow. In fact, it's so dry that it's considered a desert!

Art by Gareth Lucas

Supercool Animals

Different animals can be found in the Arctic and Antarctica. Check out a few from each spot:

The Arctic	Antarctica
• Narwhals	• Penguins
• Walruses	• Southern fur seals
• Polar bears	• Snow petrels

Bird Builders

These penguins are constructing the perfect igloo home in Antarctica! Find the eight hidden objects in this scene.

Art by Gary LaCoste

Pairs of gentoo penguins build nests together out of rocks and pebbles.

ship

sticky bun

drinking glass

ring

baseball bat

fish

pin

worm

Arctic Animal Patterns

Find and circle each pattern below in the grid.

1.

2.

3.

In this puzzle, you can see a caribou, narwhal, polar bear, puffin, walrus, and snowy owl.

Art by Erin Hunting

Make a Snowy Owl

Use household items to create your own snowy owl.

You Need
- Newspaper
- Plain newsprint paper
- Rubber band
- Scissors
- Black felt
- Orange felt
- Glue
- 2 small plastic lids

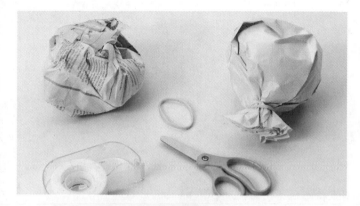

1 Crumple.

Crumple a sheet of newspaper. Then wrap a piece of plain paper around the ball. Secure extra paper with a rubber band. Cut off any excess paper.

2 Cut.

Using newspaper, cut out the owl's wings in an acorn shape.

3 Cut.

Cut two quarter-sized circles from black felt. Cut one small triangle from the orange felt.

4 Glue.

Glue the wings to the sides of the owl. Glue the black circles to the plastic lids. Glue the lids on the ball. Glue on the beak.

Penguin Path

Help the penguin at the top of the glacier slide from START to FINISH.

Penguins don't fly, but they are great swimmers. Emperor penguins can dive underwater for nearly 30 minutes at a time!

Start

Finish

Art by Dan McGeehan

Draw a Penguin

Follow the steps to learn how to sketch a penguin.

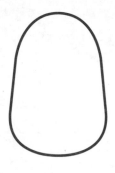 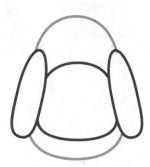  

Art by Laura Zarrin

Busy Bears

Snowball fights, snacking, and sliding—these polar bears have a lot going on! Find the eight hidden objects in this scene.

acorn

crescent moon

banana

piece of popcorn

ice pop

tack

eyeglasses

adhesive bandage

Art by Brian Michael Weaver

Adult male polar bears can stand nearly 10 feet tall on their hind legs.

Snowflake Search

No two snowflakes are alike . . . except here!
Can you find the two matching snowflakes below?

Art by iStock/ulimi

More Polar Fun!

USE YOUR STICKERS for this activity.

Caribou

Walrus

Snowy Owl

Feathers cover a snowy owl's feet to keep them warm.

Albatross

Polar Bear

Meet some animals you might see in the polar regions. Match your stickers in the back of the book to the correct pictures here.

Puffins can hold more than 10 fish in their mouths at once.

Puffin

Narwhal

Penguin

Orca

Spotted Seal

Bowhead Whale

Welcome to THE MOUNTAINS

A mountain is a big chunk of land that rises into the sky. It often has a pointed top and sloped sides. Mountains are usually found in groups called ranges. Some mountains form after pieces of Earth's crust smash into each other, pushing up land. Others form from volcanic eruptions. **Let's go for a trek in the mountains!**

Famous Mountains
- Mount Everest in Asia
- Mount Kilimanjaro in Africa
- Denali in North America
- Mount Aconcagua in South America
- Mount Fuji in Asia
- The Matterhorn in Europe

Art by Mike Moran

Llama Mama

This llama needs his mama! Can you help the baby llama find a path to her?

Llamas are native to the Andes Mountains in South America.

Llamas are part of the camel family.

Finish

Start

Art by Anna Jones

First Flight

These baby eagles are ready to leave the nest and explore the mountains. Find the eight hidden objects in this scene.

candle

drumstick

sailboat

wishbone

Art by Brian Michael Weaver

Baby eagles are called eaglets.

mitten

crown

comb

fish

Mountain Words

Trace the letters to write the names of five things you might find in the mountains.

Peak

Slope

Cliff

Summit

Rock

Silly Slopes

Mount Everest is the world's tallest mountain above sea level.

There are mountains under the sea called seamounts.

Art by Sean Parkes

Yak Snack

These yaks are digging into their grass cake.
Find the eight hidden objects in this scene.

crown

key

fried egg

gown

ruler

Wild yaks live in the Himalayas, a mountain range in Asia.

Art by Tamara Petrosino

worm

arrow

ski

Yak Match

This is a whole lot of yaks!
Can you find the two yaks in the group that are exactly the same?

More Mountain Fun!

USE YOUR STICKERS for this activity.

Mountain Goat

Yak

Peregrine Falcon

Peregrine falcons can dive faster than 200 miles an hour.

Bighorn Sheep

Black Bear

Meet some animals you might see in the mountains. Match your stickers in the back of the book to the correct pictures here.

Snow Leopard

Red Panda

Chinchilla

Panda

Llama

A newborn panda is about the size of a stick of butter.

Welcome to THE SAVANNA

Two lion cubs romp in the grass. In the distance, a giraffe munches on tree leaves. And just beyond, an elephant splashes into a water hole. We're in the savanna! A savanna is a large, warm, grassy area with trees scattered across it. **Let's go search the savanna!**

The Serengeti in eastern Africa is one of the most famous savanna regions.

Art by Eric Barclay

Baby Elephant

Eli wants to catch up with his mama.
Can you help him find a path back to her?

African elephants are the largest land animals on Earth!

Start

Finish

Art by Tim Beaumont

Swimming Along

Lions live together in groups called prides.

These animals are going for a dip!
Can you find at least 10 differences between these two pictures?

Why Do Lions Have Manes?

Most adult male lions have manes. Scientists aren't exactly sure why. But many think the lions use their manes to get the attention of female lions.

Art by Ivanke and Lola

Giraffe Match

Can you find a match for each giraffe below?

Giraffes have the same number of neck bones as humans!

Giraffes are the tallest animals on Earth.

Draw an Elephant

Follow the steps to learn how to sketch an elephant.

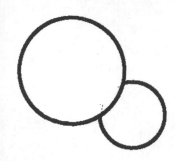  

Art by Kevin Zimmer

Hide-and-Seek

Will this bird be able to find her hiding friends?
Find the eight hidden objects in this scene.

piece of
popcorn

crown

baseball
bat

flag

fried egg

slice of pizza

ice-cream cone   boomerang

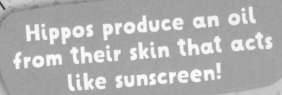
Hippos produce an oil from their skin that acts like sunscreen!

Art by Bill Golliher

Savanna Words

Trace the letters to write the names of five things you might find in the savanna.

Grass

Lion

Hippo

Zebra

Shrub

More Savanna Fun!

USE YOUR STICKERS for this activity.

Cheetah

Rhinoceros

A group of rhinos can be called a crash.

Pangolin

Zebra

Hippo

Meet some animals you might see in the savanna. Match your stickers in the back of the book to the correct pictures here.

Ostriches are the largest birds on Earth.

Ostrich

Impala

Hyena

Warthog

Baboon

Giraffe

Lion

Help
≥ THE PLANET! ≤

Earth is our home. It's a great place to live! Our planet is full of amazing habitats and wildlife. It's important to protect Earth. And there are many ways to help. Find out different things you can do to keep our home healthy. **Ready, set, go!**

Ways to Help Earth

Check out some ways to make a difference!

Use a reusable water bottle. 	Turn off lights when you leave a room. 	Make toys or games out of recycled items. 
Walk or ride somewhere you'd normally drive. 	Learn something new about the planet. 	Collect rainwater to water a plant. 
Turn off the water when brushing your teeth. 	Recycle items that you can. 	Only take what you'll eat. 

Answers

▼ Page 3

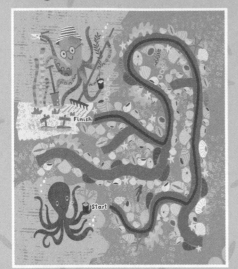

▼ Page 4

▼ Page 8

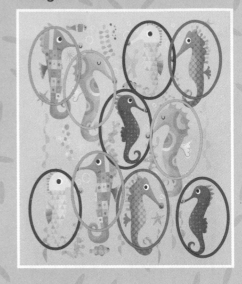

▼ Page 10

▼ Page 15

▼ Page 16

▼ Pages 18–19

Answers

▼ Page 23

▼ Page 24

▼ Page 26

▼ Pages 28–29

▼ Page 30

▼ Page 35

▼ Page 38

▼ Page 39

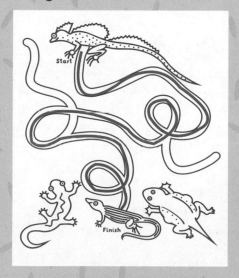

▼ Pages 40–41

Answers

▼ Page 45

▼ Page 46

▼ Page 48

▼ Page 50

▼ Page 51

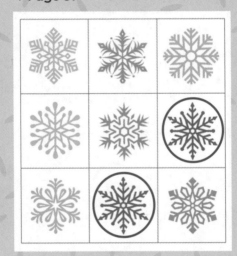

▼ Page 55

▼ Page 56

▼ Page 60

▼ Page 61

Answers

▼ Page 65

▼ Pages 66–67

▼ Page 68

▼ Page 70

Published by Highlights Press
815 Church Street, Honesdale, Pennsylvania 18431
ISBN: 978-1-63962-077-7
Manufactured in Mattoon, IL, USA
Mfg. 05/2023
First edition
Visit our website at Highlights.com.
Cover art by Gareth Lucas
Craft photos by Jim Filipski, Guy Cali Associates, Inc.
Art on pg. 75 by DigitalVision Vectors/Getty Images/jamtoons (light switch, planet); iStock/Getty Images/redchocolatte (recycling symbol, water bottle, toothbrush, plant, utensils, bike); iStock/Getty Images/Natasha_Pankina (box); iStock/Getty Images/topform84 (scissors)

Pages 12–13 More Ocean Fun!

Pages 20–21 More Forest Fun!

Pages 32–33 More Rainforest Fun!

Highlights

Pages 42–43 More Desert Fun!

Pages 62–63 More Mountain Fun!

Pages 52–53 More Polar Fun!

Pages 72–73 More Savanna Fun!

Highlights